How To Talk To Strangers

Guild in Building Meaningful Connections for Businesses and Relationships

Joseph M. Gibson

TABLE OF CONTENT

Introduction 7

CHAPTER 1 9

The Power of Connecting with Strangers 9

The Benefits of Engaging with New People 9

How Talking to Strangers Impacts Businesses and Relationships 11

CHAPTER 2 13

Overcoming Social Barriers: Building Confidence and Breaking the Ice 13

Boosting Self-Confidence in Social Interactions 13

Approaching Strangers with Ease and Authenticity 15

CHAPTER 3 17

Effective Communication Skills: Nurturing Business Connections 17

Developing Active Listening Techniques 17

CHAPTER 4 21

Finding Common Ground: Establishing Meaningful Connections in Business 21

DISCOVERING SHARED INTERESTS AND GOALS
.... 21

Networking Strategies for Business Success 23

CHAPTER 5 25

Transitioning From Small Talk To Meaningful Conversations 25

TECHNIQUES FOR ENGAGING AND DEEPENING CONVERSATIONS 25

Connecting on a Deeper Level in Business Settings 27

CHAPTER 6 29

Cultural Intelligence: Navigating Diversity in Business Relationships 29

Respecting and Appreciating Cultural Differences 29

Adapting Communication Styles for Successful Cross-Cultural Interactions 31

CHAPTER 7 33

The Art of Persuasion: Influencing and Negotiating with Strangers 33

Effective Persuasion Techniques in Business 33

Building Strong Negotiation Skills for Positive Outcomes

.... 35

CHAPTER 8 37

Safety and Boundaries: Protecting Yourself in Business Interactions.. 37

Trusting Your Instincts and Setting Boundaries 37

Ensuring Safety and Security in Professional Relationships.. 39

CHAPTER 9 41

Strengthening Personal Relationships: Connecting with Strangers on a Deeper Level 41

Enhancing Intimacy and Trust in Romantic Relationships

.... 41

Building Lasting Friendships with New Acquaintances 43

CHAPTER 10 47

Overcoming Relationship Challenges: Communication and Conflict Resolution 47

Effective Communication Strategies for Healthy Relationships.. 47

Resolving Conflicts and Nurturing Strong Bonds 50

CHAPTER 11 53

Building Bridges: Connecting with Strangers for Personal
Growth 53

Embracing New Perspectives and Expanding Your
Worldview... 53

Overcoming Social Barriers for Personal and Professional
Development.. 56

CHAPTER 12 59

Conclusion: Embracing the Power of Meaningful
Connections... 59

The Transformative Impact of Talking to Strangers..... 59

CONCLUSION.. 65

Introduction

In our increasingly interconnected world, the ability to effectively communicate with strangers has become a valuable skill set, both in the realms of businesses and relationships. Whether it's forging new connections with potential clients, collaborators, or partners, or nurturing meaningful relationships with friends, romantic interests, or colleagues, the art of talking to strangers holds tremendous potential.

This book serves as a comprehensive guide to help you navigate the complexities of engaging with unfamiliar faces in various contexts. By embracing the power of genuine connections, you'll unlock opportunities for personal and professional growth, expand your network, and foster a deeper understanding of others.

Within these pages, you will discover practical strategies to overcome social barriers, develop effective communication skills, and find common ground with strangers. We will explore how to transition from small talk to meaningful conversations, navigate cultural differences, and leverage the art of persuasion and negotiation to achieve positive outcomes.

Moreover, we will delve into the importance of setting boundaries, ensuring safety, and building trust in both business interactions and personal relationship. Through insightful tips and real-life examples, you'll learn how to navigate relationship challenges, resolve conflicts, and strengthen bonds with strangers-turned-acquaintances.

By the end of this book, you will be equipped with the tools and knowledge to confidently approach strangers, initiate engaging conversations, and create lasting connections that can transform your business ventures and personal life. Embrace the power of talking to strangers, and unlock a world of new possibilities.

CHAPTER 1

The Power of Connecting with Strangers

The Benefits of Engaging with New People

Engaging with new people, whether they are strangers or acquaintances, offers a wide array of benefits that can enhance various aspects of our lives. While it may initially feel daunting to step out of our comfort zones and initiate conversations with unfamiliar faces, the rewards that come from these interactions are worth the initial hesitation. Here are some of the key benefits of engaging with new people.

Broadening Perspectives: Interacting with individuals from diverse backgrounds exposes us to different perspectives, cultures, and ways of thinking. It expands our worldview, challenges our assumptions, and helps us develop a more inclusive and empathetic mindset.

Learning Opportunities: Every person we encounter has a unique story and a wealth of knowledge and experiences to share. Engaging with new people allows us to learn from their expertise, gain insights into unfamiliar subjects, and acquire new skills or perspectives that can contribute to our personal and professional growth.

Networking and Professional Development: Building connections with new people can significantly expand our professional network. It opens doors to potential job opportunities, collaborations, partnerships, and mentorship. These connections can provide valuable advice, support, and guidance, and may even lead to career advancements.

Personal Growth and Self-Discovery: Engaging with new people helps us develop our social skills, build confidence, and become more adaptable to different social settings. It pushes us outside our comfort zones, fosters personal growth, and allows us to discover new interests, hobbies, and passions.

Building Lasting Relationships: Some of the most meaningful relationships in our lives can stem from chance encounters with strangers. Engaging with new people creates opportunities to form deep connections, whether they evolve into lifelong friendships, romantic relationships, or professional partnerships.

Enhanced Creativity and Innovation: Exposure to different perspectives stimulates our creativity and fuels innovative thinking. Engaging with new people can inspire fresh ideas, spark creative collaborations, and bring diverse viewpoints to problem-solving, leading to more innovative and well-rounded outcomes.

Increased Cultural Awareness: Engaging with individuals from different cultures promotes cultural understanding and appreciation. It helps us break down stereotypes, fosters a sense of global citizenship, and cultivates an environment of respect and harmony.

Personal Well-being: Engaging with new people can have a positive impact on our overall well-being. Meaningful social interactions contribute to feelings of connectedness, reduce loneliness, and improve our mental and emotional health.

By actively seeking out opportunities to engage with new people, we open ourselves up to a world of benefits that extend far beyond the initial interaction. Embracing these encounters with an open mind and genuine curiosity allows us to tap into the richness of human connections and create a more fulfilling and enriched life. So, step out of your comfort zone, strike up conversations, and embrace the countless benefits that come from engaging with new people.

How Talking to Strangers Impacts Businesses and Relationships

Engaging in conversations with strangers can have a profound impact on both businesses and personal relationships. While it may seem counterintuitive to initiate conversations with unfamiliar individuals, the benefits that arise from these interactions are significant and far-reaching.

In the realm of business, talking to strangers opens up a world of opportunities. It allows entrepreneurs and professionals to expand their networks, build connections, and discover potential clients, partners, and mentors. By engaging with new people, one can tap into fresh perspectives, gain valuable insights, and foster collaborations that drive innovation and growth. Additionally, talking to strangers in a business context enhances communication skills, adaptability, and the ability to navigate diverse professional environments.

When it comes to personal relationships, talking to strangers can lead to meaningful connections and enriching experiences. It provides an avenue to meet new friends, explore romantic possibilities, and expand social circles. Engaging with strangers encourages us to step outside our comfort zones, embrace diversity, and learn from different perspectives. These interactions can deepen empathy, strengthen interpersonal skills, and cultivate a sense of belonging and community.

Furthermore, talking to strangers in both business and personal relationships nurtures personal growth. It challenges preconceived notions, broadens horizons, and fosters a deeper understanding of the world. By engaging with a diverse range of individuals, we become more open-minded, adaptable, and culturally aware.

It is important to approach these conversations with authenticity, respect, and genuine interest. By actively listening, asking meaningful questions, and fostering mutual understanding, the impact of talking to strangers can be profound. So, embrace the power of connecting with strangers, whether in business or relationships, and unlock the untapped potential that lies within these interactions.

CHAPTER 2

Overcoming Social Barriers: Building Confidence and Breaking the Ice

Boosting Self-Confidence in Social Interactions

Self-confidence plays a crucial role in our ability to navigate social interactions with ease and grace. It is the key that unlocks our potential to connect, communicate, and form meaningful relationships. Fortunately, there are strategies that can help boost self-confidence in social settings.

Firstly, it's important to practice self-acceptance and embrace your unique qualities. Recognize that everyone has insecurities and that you are worthy of genuine connections. Focus on your strengths and celebrate your accomplishments, which will help build a solid foundation of self-confidence.

Secondly, preparation can alleviate anxiety and boost self-assurance. Prior to social interactions, engage in self-reflection and identify conversation topics of interest.

Stay informed about current events, pop culture, or subjects relevant to the situation. This knowledge will give you confidence to contribute to conversations and engage others.

Additionally, maintaining positive body language and practicing good posture can greatly enhance self-confidence. Standing tall, making eye contact, and smiling create an approachable and confident demeanor. Remember, non-verbal communication is just as important as verbal communication.

Lastly, stepping out of your comfort zone and gradually exposing yourself to new social experiences can boost self-confidence over time. Start with smaller, low-pressure social situations and gradually challenge yourself to engage in larger gatherings or public speaking events.

By implementing these strategies and recognizing your own self-worth, you can boost self-confidence in social interactions. Remember, self-confidence is a skill that can be developed and refined with practice and perseverance. Embrace the opportunities to connect with others, trust in yourself, and watch your social interactions flourish.

Approaching strangers can be intimidating, but with the right mindset and approach, it can also be a rewarding and enriching experience. The key lies in embracing ease and authenticity in your interactions.

Firstly, it's important to cultivate a positive and open mindset. Approach strangers with genuine curiosity and a non-judgmental attitude. Remind yourself that everyone has unique stories and perspectives to share.

Secondly, be mindful of your body language and non-verbal cues. Maintain an open posture, make eye contact, and offer a warm smile. These signals convey approachability and help establish a friendly connection from the start.

Thirdly, start conversations with a genuine and relevant opener. It could be a simple observation, a shared interest, or a compliment. By showing interest in the other person, you create a comfortable and engaging environment.

Moreover, active listening is essential. Pay attention to the person's responses, ask follow-up questions, and show genuine interest in what they have to say.

This demonstrates your authenticity and creates a space for meaningful dialogue.

Lastly, remember that not every interaction will lead to a deep connection, and that's okay. Approach each encounter as an opportunity to learn, grow, and expand your social horizons. Embrace the experience itself rather than focusing solely on the outcome.

By approaching strangers with ease and authenticity, you open yourself up to new connections, diverse perspectives, and a world of possibilities. Embrace the beauty of human interaction, step out of your comfort zone, and watch as your social interactions become more enriching and fulfilling.

CHAPTER 3

Effective Communication Skills: Nurturing Business Connections

Developing Active Listening Techniques

Active listening is a powerful skill that can enhance your communication abilities and foster deeper connections with others, It entails listening intently to the speaker, comprehending what they are saying, and intelligently answering. Here are some key techniques to develop active listening:

Firstly, give your undivided attention to the speaker. Maintain eye contact, eliminate distractions, and genuinely focus on what they are saying. This shows respect and signals your interest in their thoughts and feelings.

Secondly, practice empathy and try to understand the speaker's perspective. Put yourself in their shoes, listen for underlying emotions, and validate their experiences. This creates a supportive environment and encourages open dialogue.

Thirdly, provide verbal and non-verbal cues to show your engagement. Nodding, smiling, and using affirming statements like "I see" or "I understand" demonstrate that you are actively listening and encourages the speaker to continue sharing.

Additionally, ask clarifying questions to ensure comprehension. Paraphrasing their points or summarizing the conversation so far helps to confirm your understanding and allows the speaker to clarify any misunderstandings.

Lastly, avoid interrupting or rushing to respond. Give the speaker space to express themselves fully before offering your input. This exhibits respect and makes it possible for a deeper discussion of the issues at hand.

By developing active listening techniques, you can deepen your connections with others, improve your communication skills, and build stronger relationships. Remember, listening is not just about hearing words; it's about understanding, empathizing, and fostering a genuine connection with those around you.

Developing Relationships and Trust with Customers and Colleagues

Rapport and trust are vital components of successful professional relationships. When clients and colleagues feel a sense of trust and connection, collaboration becomes more effective, and business relationships flourish. Here are some strategies for building rapport and trust:

Firstly, effective communication is key. Actively listen to clients and colleagues, demonstrate empathy, and show genuine interest in their perspectives. Clear and transparent communication builds a foundation of trust and understanding.

Secondly, deliver on your commitments. Consistently meeting deadlines, following through on promises, and delivering quality work establishes reliability and credibility, fostering trust in your professional relationships.

Thirdly, be authentic and genuine. Show your true self and be transparent about your intentions and capabilities. Authenticity creates an environment where trust can thrive, as it promotes honesty and openness.

Moreover, be proactive in offering support and assistance. Taking the initiative to help others demonstrates your commitment to their success and builds rapport based on mutual collaboration.

Lastly, respect boundaries and maintain confidentiality. Demonstrating discretion and confidentiality establishes trust and shows that you can be trusted with sensitive information.

By employing these strategies, you can establish strong rapport and trust with clients and colleagues. Remember, building relationships takes time and effort, but the trust and rapport you develop will be invaluable in fostering successful professional connections.

CHAPTER 4

Finding Common Ground: Establishing Meaningful Connections in Business

DISCOVERING SHARED INTERESTS AND GOALS

Shared interests and goals form the foundation of meaningful connections and collaborations. When we find common ground with others, it becomes easier to build rapport, foster teamwork, and create positive working relationships. Here are some key points to consider when discovering shared interests and goals:

Firstly, actively engage in conversations to explore common areas of interest. Ask open-ended questions, listen attentively, and find common threads that resonate with both parties. Shared hobbies, passions, or professional aspirations can create a strong bond.

Secondly, be open to diverse perspectives and experiences. Embrace the opportunity to learn from others and explore new interests. The more open-minded we are, the more likely we are to discover unexpected shared goals and forge connections.

Thirdly, participate in group activities or projects that align with your interests. This provides a platform to collaborate with like-minded individuals and work towards common objectives.

Moreover, be proactive in sharing your own interests and goals. By openly expressing your passions and ambitions, you invite others to do the same, creating an environment conducive to discovering shared aspirations.

Lastly, actively seek opportunities for mutual growth and support. Collaborate on projects, attend workshops or events together, and celebrate each other's achievements. These shared experiences foster a sense of camaraderie and strengthen the bond.

By discovering shared interests and goals, we create a sense of unity and purpose in our personal and professional relationships. Embracing diverse perspectives, actively participating in conversations, and seeking opportunities for collaboration, we can forge connections that are both fulfilling and rewarding.

Networking is an essential component of building a successful business and fostering professional growth. It provides opportunities to expand your reach, form valuable connections, and open doors to new possibilities. Here are some effective networking strategies for business success:

Firstly, attend industry events, conferences, and seminars. These gatherings offer a platform to meet like-minded professionals, exchange ideas, and forge meaningful connections.

Secondly, leverage social media platforms to expand your network. Engage in industry-related discussions, join professional groups, and actively participate in online communities to connect with individuals in your field.

Thirdly, cultivate genuine relationships by offering value and support to others. Share your expertise, provide insights, and offer assistance whenever possible. Building a reputation as a helpful and reliable professional enhances your networking efforts.

Moreover, establish a strong online presence through a professional website or blog. Showcase your skills, expertise, and achievements to attract potential collaborators and clients.

Lastly, follow up and maintain connections. Regularly reach out to contacts, attend networking events, and stay engaged in your industry. Consistency in networking efforts helps to build long-lasting relationships.

By implementing these networking strategies, you can expand your professional network, create valuable partnerships, and unlock new opportunities for business success. Remember, effective networking is not just about collecting contacts but building meaningful relationships based on mutual support and collaboration.

CHAPTER 5

Transitioning From Small Talk To Meaningful Conversations

Engaging in meaningful conversations is a powerful way to connect with others and foster deeper relationships. It allows for the exchange of ideas, perspectives, and emotions. Here are some techniques to help you engage and deepen your conversations:

Firstly, it's important to actively listen. Keep looking at the speaker, focus on them, and pay close attention. In order to show that you are truly interested in the conversation, nod, make affirming statements, and ask follow-up questions.

Secondly, practice empathy and understanding. Try to put yourself in the other person's position and consider the situation from their viewpoint. and try to see things from their perspective. This creates a safe space for open and honest communication, allowing for deeper connections.

Thirdly, be curious and ask open-ended questions. Encourage the speaker to share more about their thoughts, experiences, and feelings. Open-ended questions invite longer and more meaningful responses, leading to richer conversations.

Moreover, share your own thoughts and experiences. By being open and vulnerable, you encourage others to do the same, creating a deeper level of trust and connection.

Lastly, be mindful of non-verbal cues. Pay attention to someone's facial expressions, tone of voice, and body language. Non-verbal cues can convey emotions and intentions, enhancing the understanding and depth of the conversation.

By implementing these techniques, you can engage in more meaningful and fulfilling conversations. Building strong connections through deep conversations allows for personal and professional growth, fostering genuine relationships based on understanding and empathy.

In business settings, connecting on a deeper level with colleagues, clients, and partners is essential for building strong relationships and fostering success. Here are some key strategies for connecting on a deeper level in business:

Firstly, prioritize authenticity. Be genuine and true to yourself in your interactions. Show your personality, values, and interests. Authenticity creates a sense of trust and openness, allowing for deeper connections to form.

Secondly, actively listen and demonstrate empathy. Truly hearing and understanding others' perspectives fosters a deeper level of connection. Validate their experiences, show empathy, and respond thoughtfully to their concerns or ideas.

Thirdly, find common ground and shared goals. Identify shared interests, values, or objectives to create a sense of unity and collaboration. Working towards common goals strengthens relationships and fosters a deeper sense of purpose.

Moreover, go beyond business discussions. Take the time to get to know people on a personal level. Show genuine interest in their lives, hobbies, and aspirations. This human connection creates a stronger bond and fosters trust.

Lastly, invest in meaningful interactions. Instead of superficial small talk, engage in deeper conversations that explore ideas, challenges, and aspirations. Encourage open dialogue, exchange insights, and offer support.

By implementing these strategies, you can connect on a deeper level in business settings, fostering stronger relationships, enhancing collaboration, and creating a more fulfilling work environment.

CHAPTER 6

Cultural Intelligence: Navigating Diversity in Business Relationships

Respecting and Appreciating Cultural Differences

In our increasingly interconnected world, it is crucial to respect and appreciate cultural differences. Embracing diversity not only enriches our personal lives but also enhances our interactions in professional settings. Here are some key points to consider when it comes to respecting and appreciating cultural differences:

Firstly, develop cultural awareness and sensitivity. Educate yourself about different cultures, customs, traditions, and norms. Recognize that what may be acceptable in one culture may not be in another. Avoid assumptions and stereotypes, and approach cultural differences with an open mind.

Secondly, practice active listening and empathy. When engaging with individuals from different cultures, listen attentively and seek to understand their perspectives.

Be sensitive to their unique experiences, challenges, and values. Cultivate empathy by putting yourself in their shoes and appreciating their point of view.

Thirdly, embrace diversity in your personal and professional relationships. Foster an inclusive environment where everyone feels valued and respected, regardless of their cultural background. Encourage open dialogue and create opportunities for individuals to share their cultural experiences.

Moreover, celebrate cultural diversity through learning and sharing. Engage in cultural exchange programs, attend multicultural events, and participate in activities that promote understanding and appreciation of different cultures. By actively engaging in these experiences, we can broaden our horizons and deepen our appreciation for the richness of diverse cultures.

Lastly, practice humility and show respect. Recognize that you may not always understand or agree with cultural practices or beliefs, but it is important to approach them with respect and without judgment. Treat others with dignity and courtesy, regardless of their cultural background.

By respecting and appreciating cultural differences, we foster a more inclusive and harmonious society. Embracing diversity allows us to learn from one another, break down barriers, and create meaningful connections that transcend cultural boundaries.

Adapting Communication Styles for Successful Cross-Cultural Interactions

In our globalized world, effective cross-cultural communication is key to building successful relationships and collaborations. Adapting our communication styles to accommodate cultural differences is essential for fostering understanding and achieving meaningful connections. Here are some strategies to consider when engaging in cross-cultural interactions:

Firstly, be mindful of language barriers. Recognize that not everyone may have the same level of proficiency in a shared language. Use clear and concise language, avoid jargon or slang, and be patient when communicating with non-native speakers. Consider using visual aids or alternative communication methods when necessary.

Secondly, respect cultural norms and etiquette. Different cultures have unique communication customs and expectations. Be attentive to non-verbal cues, such as body language and personal space, as they can vary across cultures. Adapt your communication style to align with cultural preferences, showing respect and understanding.

Thirdly, practice active listening and ask clarifying questions. Understand that cultural differences can influence how information is conveyed and received. Be attentive, listen actively, and seek clarification to ensure mutual understanding. Avoid making assumptions and be open to different perspectives.

Moreover, be aware of hierarchy and power dynamics. In some cultures, authority and status play a significant role in communication. Adjust your approach accordingly, showing appropriate respect and deference to individuals in positions of authority.

Lastly, cultivate cultural intelligence. Continuously educate yourself about different cultures, their values, beliefs, and communication styles. Embrace a mindset of curiosity and learn from the experiences of others. Adapt your communication style to bridge cultural gaps and foster effective communication.

By adapting our communication styles to accommodate cultural differences, we enhance our ability to connect, collaborate, and build successful relationships across cultures. Embracing cultural diversity and practicing effective cross-cultural communication enriches our personal and professional experiences, fostering mutual respect and understanding.

CHAPTER 7

The Art of Persuasion: Influencing and Negotiating with Strangers

Effective Persuasion Techniques in Business

In the realm of business, effective persuasion is a valuable skill that can influence outcomes, drive decision-making, and achieve desired results. Whether it's convincing clients to choose your product or service, rallying support from stakeholders, or negotiating with business partners, mastering persuasion techniques is essential. Here are some key strategies to employ for effective persuasion in a business context:

Firstly, understand your audience. Tailor your message and approach to resonate with the specific needs, interests, and priorities of your target audience. Research their preferences, motivations, and pain points, and craft persuasive arguments that address their concerns and offer viable solutions.

Secondly, establish credibility and trust. Build a solid foundation by demonstrating expertise, reliability, and integrity. Share success stories, testimonials, or relevant data that validate your claims and inspire confidence. Establishing trust is crucial for others to be receptive to your persuasive efforts.

Thirdly, utilize compelling storytelling techniques. Frame your message in a narrative that captivates and engages your audience emotionally. Tell stories that evoke empathy, illustrate real-life examples, or demonstrate the positive impact of your proposal. Stories have a powerful effect on influencing decisions.

Moreover, employ evidence-based reasoning. Support your arguments with facts, statistics, case studies, or expert opinions. Data-driven arguments provide credibility and demonstrate the feasibility and benefits of your proposition.

Furthermore, use persuasive language and rhetoric. Choose words and phrases that are compelling, persuasive, and tailored to your audience. Highlight the value proposition, emphasize benefits, and address potential objections in a persuasive and convincing manner.

Lastly, employ the principles of reciprocity, scarcity, and social proof. Offering incentives or exclusive opportunities, showcasing scarcity, and highlighting others' positive experiences and endorsements can enhance your persuasive efforts.

By mastering effective persuasion techniques in business, you can influence decision-making, gain buy-in from stakeholders, and achieve your desired outcomes. Remember to understand your audience, build credibility, utilize storytelling, provide evidence, employ persuasive language, and leverage psychological principles. These strategies will strengthen your ability to persuade and drive success in the business arena.

Negotiation skills are crucial in various aspects of life, particularly in the business world. The ability to effectively negotiate can lead to positive outcomes, including successful deals, collaborations, and mutually beneficial agreements. Here are key strategies for building strong negotiation skills:

Firstly, prepare thoroughly. Before entering a negotiation, gather relevant information, understand your objectives, and anticipate potential challenges. Research the other party's interests, needs, and priorities to identify common ground and areas for compromise.

Secondly, foster effective communication. Clearly articulate your position, actively listen to the other party's perspective, and seek to understand their underlying interests. Practice empathy and maintain open-mindedness to build rapport and facilitate constructive dialogue.

Thirdly, aim for win-win solutions. Strive for outcomes that benefit both parties, as this leads to sustainable and long-term relationships. Look for creative options that address the interests of all involved and explore collaborative problem-solving.

Moreover, be adaptable and flexible. Negotiations often require adjustments and concessions. Be willing to explore alternative approaches and be open to innovative solutions that meet both parties' needs.

Furthermore, develop your emotional intelligence. Understand and manage your emotions, as well as recognize and respond to the emotions of others. This allows for better understanding and effective navigation of potential conflicts during negotiations.

Additionally, practice effective persuasion and influence techniques. Utilize persuasive language, provide compelling arguments supported by evidence, and seek opportunities to build trust and credibility.

Lastly, be patient and maintain a positive mindset. Negotiations can be complex and time-consuming, so patience is essential. Stay focused on the desired outcome and approach the process with a problem-solving attitude.

By honing your negotiation skills, you can foster positive outcomes and build strong relationships in the business realm. Through preparation, effective communication, win-win solutions, adaptability, emotional intelligence, persuasive techniques, and a positive mindset, you can navigate negotiations successfully and achieve mutually beneficial agreements.

CHAPTER 8

Safety and Boundaries: Protecting Yourself in Business Interactions

Trusting Your Instincts and Setting Boundaries

Trusting your instincts and setting boundaries are essential elements of personal growth, self-care, and maintaining healthy relationships. Instincts, often referred to as our gut feelings or intuition, serve as powerful guiding forces that can help us make decisions, navigate uncertainties, and protect ourselves from potential harm. Learning to trust and listen to our instincts can lead to better choices and outcomes in various aspects of life.

Setting boundaries is equally important. Boundaries are personal limits and guidelines that define how we want to be treated and what behaviors are acceptable to us. They create a framework for healthy interactions, establishing mutual respect, and safeguarding our emotional, mental, and physical well-being. By setting clear boundaries, we communicate our needs, values, and expectations to others, empowering ourselves to maintain healthy relationships and protect ourselves from negativity, manipulation, or exploitation.

Trusting your instincts and setting boundaries go hand in hand. When you trust your instincts, you are better equipped to recognize when your boundaries are being violated or compromised. Your instincts can alert you to red flags or warning signs in relationships or situations, prompting you to establish and enforce appropriate boundaries to protect yourself.

By cultivating trust in your instincts and setting healthy boundaries, you honor your own needs, values, and intuition. This self-awareness and self-care contribute to improved self-esteem, increased confidence, and healthier relationships built on mutual respect. Remember, trusting your instincts and setting boundaries are empowering acts that support your overall well-being and help create a positive and balanced life.

Safety and security are paramount in professional relationships, as they contribute to a positive and productive work environment. Creating a sense of safety and security fosters trust, collaboration, and mutual respect among colleagues and business partners. Here are key considerations for ensuring safety and security in professional relationships.

Firstly, establish clear expectations and boundaries. Clearly communicate guidelines, policies, and codes of conduct to all individuals involved. This promotes a shared understanding of acceptable behavior and helps prevent potential conflicts or misunderstandings.

Secondly, promote open and honest communication. Encourage an environment where individuals feel comfortable expressing their thoughts, concerns, or issues without fear of judgment or reprisal Effective communication requires both active listening and helpful criticism.

Thirdly, address any instances of harassment, discrimination, or inappropriate behavior promptly and effectively. Implement comprehensive policies and procedures to handle such situations, ensuring that all employees or team members feel supported and protected.

Moreover, provide training and resources on topics such as diversity, inclusion, and conflict resolution. This equips individuals with the knowledge and skills necessary to navigate diverse work environments respectfully and peacefully.

Furthermore, foster a culture of trust and confidentiality. Assure individuals that their personal and professional information will be handled with care and privacy. Establishing trust creates a safe space where individuals can share ideas and concerns openly.

Additionally, promote physical safety by ensuring a well-maintained and secure work environment. Implement safety protocols, emergency procedures, and necessary precautions to mitigate any potential risks or hazards.

Lastly, lead by example. Demonstrate respectful and ethical behavior in all professional interactions. Encourage collaboration, empathy, and fairness to create a positive and secure work atmosphere.

By prioritizing safety and security in professional relationships, organizations can cultivate a healthy and supportive work environment. Employees or team members will feel valued, motivated, and empowered to contribute their best efforts, ultimately driving productivity and success.

CHAPTER 9

Strengthening Personal Relationships: Connecting with Strangers on a Deeper Level

Enhancing Intimacy and Trust in Romantic Relationships

Intimacy and trust are the cornerstones of a healthy and fulfilling romantic relationship. They create a strong foundation of connection, vulnerability, and mutual understanding between partners. Here are key strategies for enhancing intimacy and trust in your romantic relationship.

Firstly, prioritize open and honest communication. Create a safe space where both partners can freely express their thoughts, feelings, and desires. Practice active listening and empathy to truly understand each other's perspectives. Effective communication builds trust and deepens emotional intimacy.

Secondly, cultivate trust through consistency and reliability. Be reliable and obedient to your commitments. Show up for your partner and be there for them in both good times and challenging moments. Trust is built over time by consistently demonstrating reliability and honesty.

Thirdly, foster emotional intimacy by sharing experiences, dreams, and vulnerabilities. Create opportunities for deep conversations where you can connect on a profound level. Be willing to be vulnerable and encourage your partner to do the same. Sharing your authentic selves strengthens the emotional bond and builds trust.

Moreover, prioritize quality time together. Dedicate time for shared activities, dates, and moments of connection. Disconnect from distractions and fully engage with each other. Quality time allows for deeper emotional connection and reinforces the bond between partners.

Furthermore, show appreciation and gratitude for each other. Acknowledge and celebrate the positive aspects of your partner and the relationship. Expressing gratitude fosters a positive atmosphere and strengthens the emotional connection.

Additionally, be mindful of each other's boundaries and respect them. Create a safe space where both partners feel comfortable expressing their needs and setting boundaries. Respecting boundaries builds trust and shows a commitment to each other's well-being.

Finally, keep the romance alive through small gestures of love and affection. Surprise your partner with acts of kindness, affectionate gestures, or heartfelt expressions of love. Small gestures can make a significant impact on the emotional connection and keep the relationship vibrant.

By implementing these strategies, you can enhance intimacy and trust in your romantic relationship. Remember, building and nurturing these foundations requires ongoing effort, but the rewards of a deeper, more fulfilling connection are well worth it.

Building Lasting Friendships with New Acquaintances

Creating meaningful and lasting friendships is a valuable aspect of our lives. While it may seem challenging to turn new acquaintances into lifelong friends, with some effort and intentionality, it is possible to cultivate strong and lasting bonds. Here are key strategies for building lasting friendships with new acquaintances.

Firstly, invest time and effort in getting to know each other. Actively engage in conversations and show genuine interest in their lives, experiences, and passions. Be a good listener and ask open-ended questions that encourage meaningful discussions. Building a foundation of understanding and shared experiences is essential for fostering friendship.

Secondly, find common interests and activities. Discover shared hobbies, passions, or causes that you both enjoy. Participate in activities together, whether it's joining a club, attending events, or pursuing shared goals. Engaging in activities you both love creates opportunities for deeper connection and strengthens the bond.

Thirdly, be reliable and supportive. Show up for your new friend during important moments and offer support during challenging times. Be a trustworthy confidant and maintain confidentiality. Reliability and supportiveness are crucial elements of building trust and fostering a lasting friendship.

Moreover, foster mutual respect and acceptance. Embrace and appreciate each other's differences and unique qualities. Respect boundaries and individual preferences. Creating an environment of acceptance allows the friendship to flourish authentically.

Furthermore, nurture the friendship through regular communication and quality time spent together. Stay in touch, whether it's through in-person meetings, phone calls, or online interactions. Dedicate time for shared activities, outings, and creating new memories. Consistent communication and quality time strengthen the bond and help the friendship grow.

Additionally, be proactive in maintaining the friendship. Initiate plans, suggest outings, and make an effort to stay connected. Friendships require mutual effort and investment from both sides. Taking the initiative shows your commitment to the friendship and ensures its longevity.

Finally, be a supportive and caring friend. Celebrate their successes, offer a listening ear during difficult times, and provide encouragement when needed. Showing genuine care and support fosters a deeper connection and creates a solid foundation for a lasting friendship.

By following these strategies, you can build lasting friendships with new acquaintances. Remember, building strong friendships takes time and effort, but the rewards of meaningful connections and lifelong companionship are immeasurable.

CHAPTER 10

Overcoming Relationship Challenges: Communication and Conflict Resolution

Effective Communication Strategies for Healthy Relationships

Effective communication is at the core of every healthy and fulfilling relationship. It is the key to understanding, resolving conflicts, and building a strong emotional connection. Here are essential strategies for practicing effective communication in your relationships.

Firstly, practice active listening. Give your full attention to your partner and truly hear what they are saying. Avoid interrupting or jumping to conclusions. Show empathy and seek to understand their perspective. Active listening promotes understanding and creates a safe space for open dialogue.

Secondly, express yourself clearly and honestly. Use "I" statements to communicate your feelings and needs without blaming or criticizing. Be respectful and avoid defensive language. By expressing yourself clearly, you allow your partner to understand your emotions and concerns, fostering a deeper connection.

Thirdly, be mindful of non-verbal communication. Pay close attention to someone's face, speech, and body language, and facial expressions. Non-verbal cues often convey emotions and can impact the message being communicated. Be aware of your own non-verbal signals and be attentive to your partner's cues as well.

Moreover, be open to feedback and willing to compromise. Create an environment where both partners feel safe to express their thoughts and concerns. Be open to constructive criticism and be willing to find middle ground when resolving conflicts. A willingness to compromise strengthens the relationship and shows a commitment to growth.

Furthermore, be patient and practice empathy. Understand that effective communication takes time and effort. Be patient with your partner's communication style and give them space to express themselves. Show empathy by putting yourself in their shoes and acknowledging their feelings and experiences.

Additionally, choose a time when you and your partner are both relaxed and open. The discussion of delicate subjects should not be done in a hurry. Setting the right atmosphere and timing for important conversations enhances the chances of productive communication.

Finally, seek professional help when needed. If communication issues persist or become overwhelming, consider seeking guidance from a couples' therapist or relationship counselor. A trained professional can provide valuable insights and strategies for improving communication in your relationship.

By practicing these effective communication strategies, you can enhance the quality of your relationships.

Remember, healthy communication is a continuous process that requires effort, understanding, and a commitment to building strong connections with your loved ones.

Resolving Conflicts and Nurturing Strong Bonds

Conflicts are a natural part of any relationship, but how we handle them can significantly impact the strength and longevity of our bonds. Resolving conflicts in a healthy and constructive manner is crucial for nurturing strong relationships. Here are key strategies for navigating conflicts and fostering stronger bonds.

Firstly, practice effective communication. Clearly express your concerns, needs, and emotions while actively listening to your partner's perspective. Use "I" statements to avoid blame and criticism. Maintain a respectful and calm tone, even in heated moments. Effective communication allows both parties to feel heard and understood.

Secondly, seek understanding and empathy. Try to see the situation from your partner's point of view and acknowledge their feelings. Cultivating empathy helps create a compassionate and supportive environment, fostering understanding and resolution.

Thirdly, find common ground and compromise. Look for mutually beneficial solutions that address the needs and concerns of both individuals involved. Compromise allows for a win-win outcome and strengthens the bond by reinforcing cooperation and mutual respect.

Moreover, practice forgiveness and let go of grudges. Holding onto resentment only hinders the healing process. Instead, work towards forgiveness and focus on moving forward together. Forgiveness promotes emotional healing and helps rebuild trust.

Furthermore, practice active problem-solving. Break down the conflict into manageable parts and work together to find practical solutions. Brainstorm ideas, consider different perspectives, and be open to trying new approaches. Collaborative problem-solving fosters teamwork and strengthens the bond.

Additionally, prioritize open and honest dialogue. Encourage ongoing conversations about feelings, concerns, and expectations. Regular check-ins help address any emerging issues before they escalate into conflicts. Creating a safe space for open dialogue promotes trust and prevents misunderstandings.

Finally, seek professional help if needed. If conflicts persist or seem insurmountable, consider seeking the guidance of a couples' therapist or mediator. A trained professional can provide valuable insights and strategies for resolving conflicts and strengthening your bond.

By applying these strategies, you can navigate conflicts effectively and nurture stronger bonds in your relationships. Remember, conflicts can be opportunities for growth and deeper understanding, and by resolving them with care and respect, you can build a foundation of trust and mutual support.

CHAPTER 11

Building Bridges: Connecting with Strangers for Personal Growth

Embracing New Perspectives and Expanding Your Worldview

One of the most enriching aspects of connecting with strangers is the opportunity to embrace new perspectives and expand our worldview. Engaging in conversations with individuals from different backgrounds, cultures, and experiences allows us to see the world through a fresh lens and challenge our preconceived notions. Here are key reasons why embracing new perspectives is essential:

Firstly, it fosters personal growth. By opening ourselves to different viewpoints, we can broaden our understanding of the world and gain new insights. This exposure helps us develop empathy, tolerance, and cultural sensitivity.

Secondly, it promotes intellectual stimulation. Engaging with diverse perspectives sparks curiosity, encourages critical thinking, and challenges our assumptions. We become more adaptable and open-minded, enabling us to navigate complex issues with a broader perspective.

Furthermore, it enhances creativity and innovation. Exposing ourselves to different ideas and perspectives can inspire us to think outside the box, leading to innovative solutions and fresh approaches to problem-solving.

Moreover, it builds stronger relationships. By appreciating and valuing diverse perspectives, we create an inclusive and welcoming environment. This fosters trust, understanding, and collaboration, which are essential for building meaningful connections and fostering positive relationships.

Additionally, embracing new perspectives can lead to personal and professional opportunities. By expanding our network and connecting with a wide range of individuals, we open doors to new experiences, collaborations, and possibilities.

Lastly, it contributes to societal progress. Embracing diverse perspectives promotes social cohesion, reduces prejudice and discrimination, and paves the way for a more inclusive and equitable society.

By actively seeking out new perspectives and engaging in conversations with strangers, we can broaden our horizons, deepen our understanding, and contribute to personal, societal, and intellectual growth. Embracing new perspectives is a continuous journey that enriches our lives and fosters a more interconnected world.

Social barriers can hinder our personal and professional growth, limiting our opportunities and potential. However, by recognizing and actively working to overcome these barriers, we can unlock new levels of development and success. Here are key strategies for overcoming social barriers:

Firstly, develop self-confidence. Building self-confidence is essential for breaking through social barriers. Recognize your successes, play to your talents, and combat self-doubt. Cultivate a positive mindset and believe in your abilities, which will empower you to step out of your comfort zone and engage with others more confidently.

Secondly, improve communication skills. Effective communication is a powerful tool for overcoming social barriers. Enhance your verbal and non-verbal communication skills, actively listen, and express yourself clearly. Practice empathy and strive to understand different perspectives. Effective communication fosters stronger connections, builds trust, and breaks down barriers.

Furthermore, expand your network. Actively seek out opportunities to meet new people, whether through professional networking events, social gatherings, or online communities. Step outside your familiar circles and embrace diversity. Building a diverse network exposes you to new ideas, perspectives, and opportunities for personal and professional growth.

Moreover, embrace cultural competence. In an increasingly globalized world, cultural competence is vital for navigating social barriers. Educate yourself about different cultures, customs, and norms. Respect and appreciate diversity, and strive to be inclusive and open-minded in your interactions. Cultural competence promotes understanding, breaks down stereotypes, and fosters harmonious relationships.

Additionally, confront fears and prejudices. Identify any biases or prejudices you may hold and actively work to overcome them. Challenge your assumptions and engage in meaningful conversations that challenge your perspectives. By confronting and overcoming fears and prejudices, you can develop a more inclusive and accepting mindset.

Lastly, seek support and guidance. Overcoming social barriers can be challenging, and seeking support from mentors, coaches, or support groups can provide valuable guidance and encouragement. Surround yourself with positive influences who believe in your potential and can help you navigate social challenges.

By actively working to overcome social barriers, we can unlock our full potential for personal and professional development. Embrace self-confidence, improve communication skills, expand your network, embrace cultural competence, confront fears and prejudices, and seek support. With determination and a growth mindset, you can break through social barriers and achieve success in all aspects of your life.

CHAPTER 12

Conclusion: Embracing the Power of Meaningful Connections

The Transformative Impact of Talking to Strangers

Talking to strangers has the power to transform our lives in profound and unexpected ways. While it may initially seem daunting or uncomfortable, engaging in conversations with unfamiliar individuals can lead to remarkable personal growth, expanded perspectives, and meaningful connections. Here are key aspects highlighting the transformative impact of talking to strangers:

Firstly, it broadens our horizons. When we step outside our comfort zones and engage with people from diverse backgrounds, cultures, and experiences, we expose ourselves to new ideas, beliefs, and ways of life. This exposure challenges our preconceptions, expands our knowledge, and broadens our understanding of the world. It opens doors to new perspectives, enriching our lives and fostering a sense of empathy and inclusivity.

Secondly, it promotes personal development. Talking to strangers requires us to overcome social barriers, such as fear, shyness, or judgment. By pushing ourselves to initiate conversations, actively listen, and share our own thoughts and experiences, we develop valuable skills like communication, empathy, and self-confidence. These skills not only enhance our interactions with strangers but also have a ripple effect on our personal and professional relationships.

Furthermore, it fosters serendipity and opportunities. Some of life's most remarkable encounters and opportunities come from unexpected conversations with strangers. Engaging in dialogue with unfamiliar individuals can lead to serendipitous connections, new friendships, professional collaborations, and even life-changing experiences. By embracing the unknown and being open to serendipity, we create space for extraordinary moments and opportunities to enter our lives.

Moreover, it nurtures a sense of community. In a world where connection and belonging are increasingly vital, talking to strangers can help foster a sense of community. By initiating conversations, we break down barriers, bridge divides, and create moments of shared humanity. These interactions remind us that we are all interconnected, fostering empathy, understanding, and a sense of belonging.

Additionally, it cultivates resilience and adaptability. Engaging in conversations with strangers requires us to navigate unfamiliar territory, adapt to different communication styles, and navigate diverse perspectives. This cultivates resilience, flexibility, and the ability to navigate various social settings. As we encounter different individuals and situations, we learn to adapt, communicate effectively, and navigate the complexities of human interaction.

In conclusion, talking to strangers has the power to transform our lives in remarkable ways. By embracing the unknown, broadening our horizons, fostering personal development, nurturing a sense of community, and cultivating resilience, we open ourselves up to a world of possibilities. So, let us embrace the transformative impact of talking to strangers, for within these connections lies the potential for growth, discovery, and the profound enrichment of our lives.

Meaningful relationships are at the core of our personal and professional fulfillment. Building and nurturing these connections not only brings joy and fulfillment but also plays a crucial role in our success and well-being. Here are key aspects of cultivating and sustaining meaningful relationships:

Firstly, authenticity is the foundation. Meaningful relationships are built on genuine and authentic connections. Being true to ourselves and others allows us to establish trust, foster deeper connections, and create a safe space for open communication. Authenticity invites others to show up as their true selves, fostering a sense of belonging and fostering deeper understanding.

Secondly, effective communication is vital. Open and honest communication is key to cultivating and sustaining meaningful relationships. Active listening, empathy, and clear expression of thoughts and emotions create an environment of understanding and connection. Effective communication ensures that needs, expectations, and boundaries are respected, fostering healthy and harmonious relationships.

Furthermore, mutual respect and support are essential. Meaningful relationships thrive on mutual respect, appreciation, and support. Valuing the unique qualities, strengths, and contributions of others builds a strong foundation for long-lasting connections. Being there for one another in times of both celebration and adversity nurtures a sense of trust, reliability, and loyalty.

Moreover, investing time and effort is crucial. Building and sustaining meaningful relationships requires time and effort. It involves prioritizing and dedicating quality time to connect, engage, and nurture the relationship. Regular check-ins, meaningful conversations, and shared experiences contribute to the depth and longevity of the connection.

Additionally, shared values and goals create alignment. Meaningful relationships are often grounded in shared values, goals, or a common purpose. When individuals align on core principles and aspirations, it creates a strong bond and sense of camaraderie. This shared sense of purpose and direction fosters collaboration, synergy, and mutual growth.

In conclusion, cultivating and sustaining meaningful relationships is a vital aspect of both business and personal life. Through authenticity, effective communication, mutual respect, time investment, and alignment of values and goals, we can forge connections that bring joy, support, and fulfillment. By fostering meaningful relationships, we not only enrich our own lives but also contribute to the well-being and success of those around us. So, let us invest in the cultivation and nurturing of these connections, for they are the building blocks of a fulfilling and prosperous journey in both business and life.

CONCLUSION

In the journey of life, the power of connecting with strangers should never be underestimated. Through this guide, we have explored the importance and benefits of talking to strangers in both business and personal settings. We have discovered that engaging with new people opens doors to opportunities, expands our perspectives, and fosters personal and professional growth.

By embracing the power of connecting with strangers, we enhance our self-confidence, develop valuable communication skills, and deepen our understanding of diverse cultures and perspectives. We have learned how to build rapport, trust, and strong relationships with clients, colleagues, and romantic partners. We have explored techniques for effective persuasion, negotiation, and active listening, all of which contribute to successful interactions and positive outcomes.

Moreover, we have recognized the significance of setting boundaries, respecting cultural differences, and ensuring safety and security in our relationships. We have discovered the transformative impact of talking to strangers on personal and professional development, as well as the joy of building lasting friendships and sustaining meaningful connections.

As we conclude this guide, let us remember that connecting with strangers is not merely a casual interaction but an opportunity for growth, learning, and building bridges. It requires an open mind, empathy, and a genuine desire to understand and connect with others.

So, let us venture forth with confidence, armed with the knowledge and strategies to engage with strangers in meaningful and impactful ways. By embracing the art of talking to strangers, we unlock endless possibilities for personal and professional success, enrich our lives with diverse experiences, and contribute to a more connected and empathetic world.